SHOW-ME-HOW
I Can Experiment

Fun-to-do simple science projects for young children

STEVE & JANE PARKER

HERMES HOUSE

This edition is published by Hermes House

Hermes House is an imprint of Anness Publishing Ltd
Hermes House, 88-89 Blackfriars Road, London SE1 8HA
tel. 020 7401 2077; fax 020 7633 9499; info@anness.com
© Anness Publishing Ltd 2003

A CIP catalogue record for this book is available from
the British Library.

Publisher: Joanna Lorenz
Managing Editor, Children's Books: Sue Grabham
Project Editor: Judith Simons
Designer: Michael R. Carter
Photographer: John Freeman
Stylist: Thomasina Smith

Printed in Singapore

PLEASE NOTE
The level of adult supervision needed will
depend on the ability and age of the
child following the experiments. However,
we advise that adult supervision is always
preferable, and vital if the experiment calls
for the use of sharp knives or other objects.
See the ⚠ symbol for more information on
where adult help is needed for each experiment.

ACKNOWLEDGEMENTS
The publishers would like to thank the following
children who were such wonderful models, and
their parents: Dean Denning, Liam and Lorenzo
Green, Kirsty and Rebecca Fraser, Otis and Alex
Lindblom-Smith, Gabriella and Izabella Malewska,
and Antonino Sipiano.

Contents

Introduction

Children are very curious people. So are scientists. Both ask questions about the world around them. How does this work? What does that do? Why do things happen? And can things be improved? You may already ask grownups how things happen. What, where, when and why? This means you are already a natural scientist. Scientists find the answers to their questions by doing experiments. You can do the same. This book shows you how to do tests and experiments for yourself. Then you can find

Find out why some things float and others sink.

out the answers to your questions, like a real scientist. You can also go on to invent more experiments and do more projects. Perhaps you will make a great discovery and become famous!

Young Scientists

You have already been doing experiments for years, probably without knowing it. When you were a tiny baby, you started to move your arms and legs about. You grabbed and kicked things,

Make a sound gun with a cardboard tube and discover how sound travels.

to see what would happen. When you were bigger, you probably did experiments when you played with your toys. Could you eat them? Did they make a noise when you dropped them? Could you pull them apart to see inside? Playing is experimenting, and playing is fun, so experimenting is fun, too.

As you do the experiments in this book, you will find out about light and electricity, how water and wind work, and how heat and cold affect things. This book tells you what to do and then explains what happens. All these experiments are safe with the help of grownups. You can also make up your own experiments and find things out for yourself. In this way you will learn more about the world.

Different Kinds of Science

Science is so huge that no one can know everything about it.

Find out why things look back-to-front in a mirror.

So scientists usually specialize. This means they study just one or a few subjects. For example, medical scientists study why people become ill, and how to make them better. Biologists study animals and plants, where they live and how they grow. Chemists study chemicals and other substances, what they are made of, and how they can be changed and used. Physicists study how things move, what holds them together or pulls them apart, and how energy makes things happen. Astronomers study the planets, stars and the whole universe.

How to Do an Experiment

Whatever scientists study, they usually work in the same way. This is called the scientific method. They do not rush, and they always keep things clean and safe.

• First the scientist finds out as much as possible about the subject. This is called research. What is already known about the subject? What experiments have other scientists done, and what did they discover? Do people really know the facts, or are they just guessing?

• Then the scientist decides on a good question to ask. It should be a new question that no one has asked before. But it must not be too complicated. Most scientists find out more by working in small stages, bit by bit.

• The scientist may have an idea of the possible answer to the question. In other words, he or she may guess what will happen in the experiment. This possible answer is called a theory.

• Next, the scientist thinks of an experiment that will test the theory, to find the answer to the question. This is called planning or designing the experiment. In a good experiment, everything happens clearly and safely, and nothing can go wrong – hopefully!

• Now the scientist gathers all the bits and pieces to do the experiment. These are called the materials and equipment. Everything is set out neatly and cleanly, and labelled clearly, so that there are no mix-ups.

• At last, the scientist carries out the experiment, working carefully and safely. He or she finds out what happens by looking and listening, and perhaps by feeling or smelling. The things that happen are called the results. These are written down carefully in the Science Record Book. Everything is cleaned up and tidied away afterwards.

• Next, the scientist thinks about the results. Were they expected, or not? Is the theory right, or wrong? If the theory is right, the scientist has found something new. If the theory is wrong, the scientist can try to think of another theory, or perhaps the experiment did not work properly. Remember – no experiment is a failure. A good scientist can always learn from the results, whatever they are.

• After more experiments, the scientist will be able to gather the answers together. He or she must check everything, then check it again. Finally, the scientist may make a new discovery, and become famous.

Being a Good Scientist

Scientists are very careful people. They have to be. They often work with dangerous machines, equipment and chemicals. And science can be very costly. So scientists also need to be sure that their experiments are worthwhile, and that there will be no mistakes. So they make sure everything is thought out and prepared carefully.

When you do experiments, get the materials and equipment ready first. Have a clean, safe area to carry out your experiment in, as described over the page. And ask a grown-up to check that everything is safe.

Water is great fun to splash around, as long as you are working in a waterproof area.
Science tip For experiments with water or other liquids, see if you can do them in a large bowl, such as a washing-up bowl. This catches any splashes or spills.

Heat can be very dangerous. Hot water and steam can burn or scald your skin. And when very hot water is poured into cold jars, beakers or bowls, it can make them crack or melt. So *always* get a grown-up to help you with experiments that need hot water, and make sure your equipment can stand up to it. Cookers and kettles must only be used when a grown-up is present. Liquids can boil over suddenly, and things may catch fire without warning.

Use a jug with a spout and a funnel when pouring liquids.

Never touch electric sockets, plugs or wires.

Wear a pair of rubber gloves when handling vinegar or lemon juice.

Always ask a grown-up to cut anything with sharp scissors or a craft knife.

Science tip Put a metal teaspoon into a jar before pouring in hot water. This should stop the heat cracking the jar.

Ice can freeze skin just as badly as hot water can burn. Ice has the added danger that it sticks to dry skin. When you make ice in a freezer, get a grown-up to help you.
Science tip Use rubber or washing-up gloves when handling ice. Wet the ice and the gloves first, so they do not stick together.

Electricity from a small battery is usually safe, since there is not enough power to give a shock. Static electricity can sometimes be felt as a tingle that makes you jump, for example when it builds up on a car and you touch the handle. But the static that builds up on a balloon, as shown in this book, is too small to feel.
Science tip The electricity that is used in the home is very dangerous. It can kill! NEVER touch electric sockets, plugs or wires.

Chemicals used in this book are mostly substances used for cooking and they are harmless in normal quantities. But

Put a metal teaspoon into a jar before pouring in hot water.

good scientists know that chemicals can be dangerous if they get into the wrong place. This includes near too much heat, or inside your body if you swallow them. Never taste or eat chemicals that you are using for experiments. Always ask a grown-up to get the things you need from the kitchen cupboard. NEVER touch cleaning chemicals, medicines or alcohol.

Science tip Use rubber gloves to handle large quantities of acids like vinegar or lemon juice.

Cutting and making holes can be quite difficult. Scissors and sharp points can be dangerous if they are not used properly. So ask a grown-up to help.

Science tip Draw a line where you are going to cut with scissors, before you start cutting. It is usually easier to follow a line.

Label everything – it is the sign of a good scientist. Your experiment might be ruined if you cannot remember what you put in each jar, or if you get your chemicals mixed up. Write labels on pieces of paper or use special sticky-backed labels. Stick these in the right place, or put them under jars or beakers.

Science tip Use a pencil for your labels. Some felt-tipped pens can blot and run if splashed with water.

Your Science Record Book

All scientists record their experiments and the results. You need to know exactly what you did during an experiment, so that you can repeat it to check the result, or change it to find out something else. Each time you do an experiment, record the following information in your book. If you find writing difficult ask a grown-up to help with some of the details and draw a picture of what happened instead.

• the day and date
• the experiment's name, and the idea behind it
• how you did your experiment, perhaps with a drawing or diagram
• the results, written in words, or perhaps as a chart with ticks and crosses

You can make a Science Record Book by covering a notebook or school-type exercise book with coloured paper. The paper needs to be about 3–4 cm (1¼–1½ in) larger all around than the book when it is opened flat.

Further Research

When scientists have finished their set of experiments, they often try to find out a bit more, perhaps by changing the experiment slightly. See if you can make changes to some of your experiments to find out more. Record what you do and your results in your Science Record Book.

Your Science Record Book

1 Place the book centrally on the coloured paper, with one cover open. Turn the edges of the paper over the cover and stick them down with glue. You can snip the corners of the paper to give a neater finish. Repeat with the other cover.

2 Decorate the cover with something scientific, perhaps numbers, bubbles and shapes, drawings of test-tubes and scientific equipment, or cut-out photographs of scientific gadgets.

3 Record all the information that you have learned from your experiments. If you like, you can stick some of the things you have made in the book, to keep.

Where to Do Experiments

Many scientists work in special rooms called laboratories. There they have all the equipment, materials, tools and machines they need to do their experiments. But not all science happens in laboratories. To do research, many scientists go to libraries to read books. They visit exhibitions and museums to find out more. They also meet other scientists and talk about their work.

The Home Laboratory

You can set up your own laboratory in your home or school. It might be in a kitchen, bathroom, shed or garage. You usually need somewhere with waterproof surfaces, where there is no danger of damaging furniture or carpets. Ask a grown-up to choose the best place.

The main thing you will need is a large work surface, like a table. The place should be brightly lit and not too hot or cold. For some experiments, you will need a freezer, or a refrigerator with a freezing compartment. You will sometimes need lots of water. Warm water can come from a hot tap or a kettle. You might also need somewhere to heat up a saucepan. Always ask a grown-up to help.

Science tip Cover your work surface with several layers of old newspaper. This stops paint and food colouring staining the work surface, and will also absorb spilt liquids and glue.

Materials and Equipment

You will find most of the materials, equipment and tools that you need for your experiments around the house. Always gather everything you need and check it before you start the experiment. If you do not, you may run out of something halfway through.

If necessary, you can buy extra supplies of pencils, pens, scissors, sticky tape, paper, card, blotting paper, glue, sticky labels and shapes, poster paints and similar things from a good stationery shop or office supplier.

You can find food colourings, bicarbonate of soda, vinegar, lemon juice, milk, cocktail sticks, skewers and similar things in the kitchen.

Batteries, wires and small torch bulbs are sold in electrical, DIY or model shops. You can buy small mirrors from the chemist, and sand or gravel from a builders' supplier or a timber merchant.

Be a Green Scientist

Good scientists know that they must look after our planet by saving resources, recycling things, and not damaging the environment or causing waste and pollution. This is called being "green" since it helps to save trees, plants, flowers, animals and natural places on our planet Earth.

You can be a "green scientist" by saving, reusing and recycling things. You will also save money!

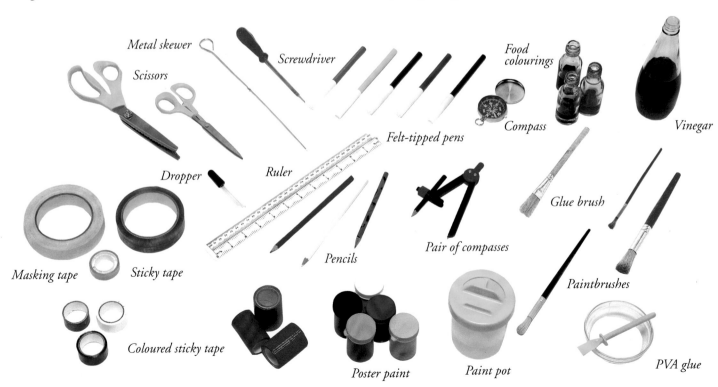

Metal skewer
Scissors
Screwdriver
Food colourings
Felt-tipped pens
Compass
Vinegar
Dropper
Ruler
Glue brush
Masking tape
Sticky tape
Pencils
Pair of compasses
Paintbrushes
Coloured sticky tape
Poster paint
Paint pot
PVA glue

Tissue paper

Plastic strainer

Wooden spoon

Jars

Bottle

Torch bulb and holder

9-volt battery

Coloured paper

Balloons

Blotting paper

Plastic cups

Sand

Modelling clay

Mirrors

Coloured stickers

Wooden skewer

Electrical wire

String

Bicarbonate of soda

• Use old newspapers, and store your equipment in empty cartons or boxes.
• The card from cereal boxes is ideal for many experiments.
• Ask grown-ups for used paper that has been written on one side – you can use the blank side.
• After picnics and parties, wash the paper or plastic cups and plates. You can use them for your experiments.
• Save the cardboard tubes from the insides of toilet rolls and kitchen rolls.
• Wash and keep empty jars for your experiments. But remember that glass is easily broken and is then very dangerous to handle.
• Save plastic drinks bottles. Carefully cut off the tops and turn them upside-down to make funnels. The lower parts make plastic jars – safer than glass ones.
• When you have finished with your equipment, take it to your local recycling centre.

Have Fun

If you follow the safety rules in this book, and carry out your experiments slowly and sensibly, you will find that science is fun. You can make some amazing discoveries, and learn lots.

Find out more by doing further research, by reading about science, and by watching science programmes. You can become an expert scientist and answer all your friends' questions. You might even make a discovery or invention that will change the world!

A Note for Grown-ups

Some of the experiments in this book can be followed by a child alone, but often adult help is needed. Always supervise your children closely whenever they are using home experiment materials. The places in the book where your assistance is vital, such as when sharp scissors or a craft knife are needed, are marked !.

Creatures of the Night

Light is bright, and when there is no light it is dark. A shadow is a patch of darkness. It is formed when something gets in the way of light beams, which can only travel in straight lines. In Alex's puppet show, some of the light from the torch shines on the wall. But the light that hits the ghostly black creatures cannot get through or round them. So the wall behind their shapes stays dark – as their shady, scary shadows.

You can make the shadows on the wall bigger or smaller. When the puppets are near the torch, they cover more of the light beam, and so the shadows on the wall are bigger, but their edges are fuzzy and blurred.

Light fantastic

Light is amazing. It comes and goes in a flash, weighs nothing, travels faster than anything else in the universe – and even scientists do not fully understand it. The light we turn on in our homes is produced by electricity. This passes through the very thin wire inside a light bulb and makes the wire glow brightly. The light beams then spread out in all directions, and always in straight lines. The light bulb in a torch has a mirror behind it to make all the light beams come out at the front only.

❗ Young children will need help cutting out card shapes with scissors and should not be allowed to handle craft knives. They might also need help in the "dark room", to hold the torch or just for company. Be sure they cannot get themselves locked in a dark room or cupboard.

YOU WILL NEED THESE MATERIALS AND TOOLS

Coloured pencil

Black card

Scissors

Straws or wooden skewers

Torch

Coloured sticky tape

Dark room with a white wall, screen or sheet

1 Draw the outlines of some night-time creatures, like bats, owls and spiders, on the black card with the pencil. Make them big.

2 Draw some stars and a moon too. Cut out the shapes carefully with scissors. If the scissors are sharp, ask a grown-up to help you.

3 Draw features such as eyes and feathers or even bone patterns onto the night-time creatures. Keep these quite simple.

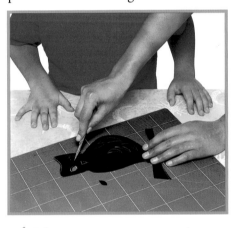

4 Ask a grown-up to cut out the eyes, feather patterns and any other details with a craft knife.

5 Stick the straws or skewers to the shapes with sticky tape to make handles.

Changing Shadows

Things that light can pass through easily, like air or glass, are called **transparent**. Solid things like your night creature cut-outs do not let any light pass through. They are **opaque**. A **translucent** substance is one that lets through some light but not all of it, like tracing paper or tissue paper. Cover one side of a cut-out animal with tissue paper. When you hold it up in front of the torch, less light will shine through the holes.

6 In a darkened room, ask a friend to shine the torch on a light wall. Move the creatures and other shapes in the torch's light, to make their ghostly shadows dance on the wall.

Mysterious Mirrors

Otis is discovering that what you see in a mirror is not an exact copy of the original thing. It is back-to-front – a mirror picture or mirror-image. His drawings and writing always look the other way round in the mirror. So does your face! The face that you see when you look in the mirror is a mirror-image. It is not the same as the face that your friends and family see when they look at you, or when you look at a photograph of yourself.

Reflections

Light beams travel in straight lines – unless they bounce off things. This bouncing is called **reflection**. Only a few things, like the Sun, light bulbs, candles and fires, give out their own light beams. These shine into our eyes and we see them. We see other things because they bounce or reflect light beams into our eyes. Very smooth, shiny surfaces like mirrors are very good at reflecting. When you look at your face in a mirror, you see light beams that have come from the Sun or an electric light to your face, bounced off it towards the mirror, and then bounced back again into your eyes!

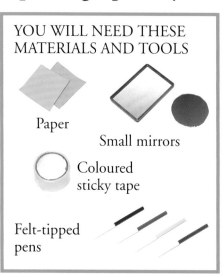

YOU WILL NEED THESE
MATERIALS AND TOOLS

Paper

Small mirrors

Coloured
sticky tape

Felt-tipped
pens

Otis is having fun making his drawings and writing turn around in a mirror. See if you can make a mirror-image come out the right way round.

1 Mirrors are made of glass or plastic. Some may have sharp edges. Ask a grown-up to put some sticky tape round them to make them safe.

2 Do a drawing and write the name of what you have drawn on a piece of paper. Be as neat as you can.

3 Hold the mirror up next to the paper. Can you read the writing in it? Does the drawing look exactly the same as it does on the paper?

4 Write the name backwards or do the drawing back-to-front. What does it look like in the mirror now?

5 Think of a whole drawing. Draw half of it, using one half of the paper only.

6 Can you make up the rest of the drawing by holding the mirror alongside it? Is the result what you had expected?

See Back to the Future!

You can make an image bounce backwards and forwards between mirrors, almost for ever. Sit behind one mirror. Hold out another mirror facing you. Look into this mirror. Move both mirrors slightly until you can see the reflection of the mirror in the reflection of the mirror in the reflection of the mirror in the reflection of the mirror and on and on.

13

Tell the Time by the Sun

When the Sun rises in the morning, it is low in the sky. It shines on objects from the side to make long, thin shadows. As the Sun moves up and across the sky, the shadows get shorter and move around. At midday the Sun is at its highest point, and the shadows are at their shortest. As the Sun continues its journey across the sky in the afternoon, the shadows get longer again, but on the other side of the objects.

Gabriella has made a sundial so that she can watch the changing shadow of the dial pointer – and tell the time by it.

Light days and dark nights

Each day, it looks as if the Sun moves across the sky. But really, the Sun stays still, and it is the Earth that moves. The Earth is like a giant ball that spins round and round. We stay in one place on the surface of the ball, so it looks to us as though the Sun is moving. When the Sun disappears at night, we are on the shadowy side of the Earth. The Sun is still shining, but on the other side. For people there, it is daytime. For us, it is night-time.

[!] Young children may need to be shown how to draw a circle with a pair of compasses, and how to use a magnetic compass to find North and South. The sundial pointer should face North, since the Sun is in the South at midday, so it throws its shadows onto the dial.

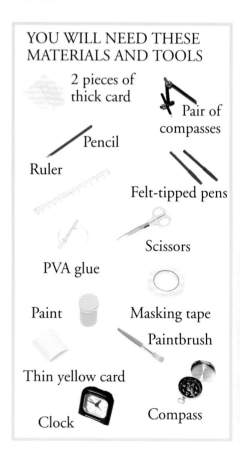

YOU WILL NEED THESE
MATERIALS AND TOOLS

2 pieces of thick card

Pair of compasses

Pencil

Ruler

Felt-tipped pens

Scissors

PVA glue

Paint

Masking tape

Paintbrush

Thin yellow card

Clock

Compass

1 Open the pair of compasses so the point is about 8 cm (3 in) from the pencil. Push the point into the middle of the thick card and turn the compasses to draw a circle.

2 Draw a square on some thick card with a felt-tipped pen and a ruler. Each side of the square should be about 8 cm (3 in). Draw a diagonal line across the square to make two triangles.

3 Carefully cut out the circle and one triangle from the card. This will be the pointer of the sundial. (You can keep the other triangle as a spare.)

4 Draw a straight line from the centre of the circle, where the compass point stuck in to it, to the edge, using the ruler.

5 Stick the triangle to the circle along the line using PVA glue. Hold the triangle in place with masking tape until the glue dries.

6 If you like, paint your sundial bright yellow. Add a smiley face and some wavy sunbeams cut out of thin yellow card.

7 Put your sundial in a safe, sunny place. Find North with the compass. Turn the sundial until the long side of the pointer points towards North. Draw a straight line at the edge of the shadow.

Right: You can make your sundial into a clock. Every hour, when the big hand on a real clock gets to 12, draw a line at the edge of the shadow. Write the time by each line.

15

Disappearing Rainbow

When sunlight or torch light shines on a wall, it looks white. But really, it is made up of many different colours – the colours of the rainbow. You can show this in two ways. One is by splitting white light into its different colours with a prism, or you can add the colours together to make white light. Gabriella is doing this by making a colourful spinning top. When she spins the top very fast all the rainbow colours blur and merge together, back into white.

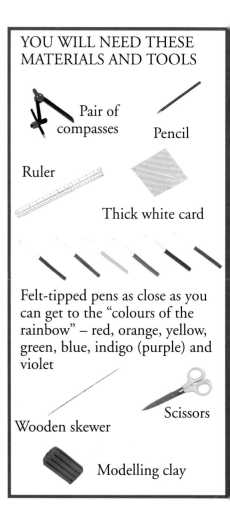

YOU WILL NEED THESE MATERIALS AND TOOLS

Pair of compasses

Pencil

Ruler

Thick white card

Felt-tipped pens as close as you can get to the "colours of the rainbow" – red, orange, yellow, green, blue, indigo (purple) and violet

Wooden skewer

Scissors

Modelling clay

Rainbows

Rainbows form in the sky when the sun shines on raindrops. The tiny raindrops bend the light beams, separating the different colours. Next time you see a rainbow, look carefully at it. Write down or colour in the colours you see in your Science Record Book. These colours are called the spectrum of light. They are always the same and always in the same order.

! Young children may need to be shown how to draw a circle with a pair of compasses and how to divide it into seven roughly equal segments. They may need help with cutting thick card and pushing in the skewer. They may also need help to spin the top fast enough for the colours to merge.

Gabriella can spin her rainbow-disc top to see how the coloured light beams blur together and mix into white light.

1 Open the pair of compasses so there is about 5 cm (2 in) between the point and the pencil. Push the point into the centre of the card and draw a circle.

2 You need to divide the circle into seven same-sized parts, like cutting a cake into seven equal slices. Using a ruler, draw seven lines with a pen or pencil, from the centre of the circle to the edge.

3 Carefully cut around the circle with the scissors to make a disc. If the card is very thick, ask a grown-up to help.

4 Colour in each "slice" with a differently coloured felt-tipped pen. Remember to follow the order of colours in the rainbow spectrum: red, orange, yellow, green, blue, indigo and violet.

5 Push the skewer through the centre of the card disc, where the compass point was, to make a spinning top. You may need help with this. Fix the skewer firmly to the disc with small blobs of modelling clay.

6 Spin the disc like a top, by rolling the skewer very fast between your finger and thumb. You may need some practice to make this work properly.

Mixing Beams

If you mixed together the ink from the coloured pens you have used for your rainbow on a piece of paper, it would make a purple-brown mess. So why do the spinning colours seem to make white? It is because when you spin the disc, it is not the inks of the pens that are mixing together. Instead, it is the coloured light beams, which are bouncing off each coloured "slice", that are mixing together.

Magic Magic-markers

When you paint a picture, do you mix lots of colours to make the exact shade of colour you need? You can make hundreds of different colours, even if you only have a few paints to start with. In fact, you need only three colours to make any other colour you want. These colours are red, blue and yellow. They are called the primary colours. You can make any other colour by mixing them, but you cannot make them by mixing any other colours. Antonino is finding out which colours of inks were mixed to make the colours of his felt-tipped pens.

Real science

In science, this experiment is calle[d] **chromatography**. It works becau[se] the water creeps up the blotting p[aper] it carries with it the different colo[ured] inks, at different speeds. Chromatography is very importan[t in] science. It is used by scientists to separate all sorts of mixtures [and] combinations, like salty s[ea] water or a piece of moo[n] rock, to find out what is really in them.

YOU WILL NEED THESE MATERIALS AND TOOLS

White blotting paper

Scissors

Water-soluble felt-tipped pens of several different colours

Jars

Water

Antonino shows that his red, yellow and blue felt-tipped pens are not what they seem. They contain mixtures of inks, of different colours.

18

1 Carefully cut the blotting paper into long strips that will fit inside the jars. Make a large ink blot about 2 cm ($^3/_4$ in) from one edge of each piece of blotting paper with a differently coloured felt-tipped pen.

2 Allow the blots to dry thoroughly. Stand each piece of blotting paper in a jar with the blot towards the bottom.

3 Very carefully pour about 1 cm ($^1/_2$ in) of water into each jar. Do not let the level of the water reach the ink blots, and try not to splash the blotting paper as you pour.

⚠ This is a fairly straightforward experiment but it might be a little messy, so cover surfaces with newspaper or provide a waterproof area. The experiment takes time to work, perhaps a few hours. But the results are clearest if the inks are not left too long, otherwise they get drawn to the edge of the paper and combine again.

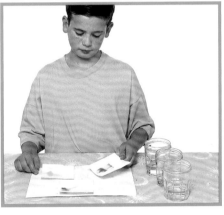

4 Check the jars every few minutes. You will see the water being soaked up by the blotting paper. When the water gets near to the top, take the blotting papers out of the jars.

Your Science Record Book

Let the strips of blotting paper dry on a newspaper and stick them in your Science Record Book. Write the colour of the felt-tipped pen you used on each strip of blotting paper, using a pencil (which is not affected by water) or by marking them with the original pen right at the top. The bands of colours on the blotting paper show the separate ink colours that were mixed together to make the colour of that pen. If the felt-tip pen was orange, green, purple or brown, there are probably lots of colour bands. If the pen was one of the primary colours – red, blue and yellow – there may be only one or two bands.

Balloon Snowstorm

Electricity is strange stuff. It is invisible, which means we cannot see it. But it is also very powerful, and it can be very dangerous. We use electricity in our homes in lots of different ways, to make things work, such as light bulbs, heaters, vacuum-cleaners, washing machines, radios and music players. This electricity is very strong. NEVER mess about with this electricity. However, you can make your own electricity, which is safe and fun. It does not move along wires and it is not as powerful as mains electricity. It is called static electricity.

Lorenzo has charged his balloon with static electricity, by rubbing it. It sticks to his T-shirt and attracts the tissue paper "snow flakes".

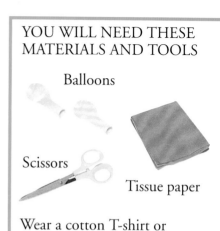

YOU WILL NEED THESE MATERIALS AND TOOLS

Balloons

Scissors

Tissue paper

Wear a cotton T-shirt or woollen jumper

Charge your balloon

Static electricity is in tiny bits, called charges. These can be **positive** or **negative**, just like the two connections on a battery (see the experiment called Battery Light Show). An object such as a balloon has an equal number of positive and negative charges over its surface. They cancel each other out, so over a whole balloon there is no static electricity. But when a balloon is rubbed against a different material, such as a T-shirt, some of the positive charges go onto the T-shirt and stay there. This leaves extra negative charges on the balloon, which make it "sticky".

Making static electricity is easier on cold, dry days. On warm, humid days, the air itself is full of static. Children might need help blowing up and tying balloons.

1 Blow up a balloon quite hard and tie the neck. Do not blow your balloon up so much that it bursts. But make sure it is fairly hard, since a soft, squashy balloon does not work so well.

2 Make some "snow" by tearing or cutting tissue paper into little bits. If you have the time, you could make each "flake" a pointed star with six sides, like real snow flakes.

3 Rub the balloon several times on your T-shirt or woolly sweater. Rub it quite fast until the balloon tries to "stick" to the T-shirt or sweater. The balloon is now charged with static electricity.

4 Hold the balloon near the "snow". The flakes are lifted up by the static electricity on the balloon. After a little while, the electricity leaks away and the flakes fall softly.

5 Rub your balloon again to re-charge it, then hold it near a friend's hair and see what happens. For the best effect, choose someone with longish hair.

Push and Pull

There are two types of static electricity charge, positive and negative. Charges which are different attract, or pull each other together. So the balloon sticks to anything with the opposite charge, even water. Lorenzo is holding a charged balloon near a stream of water. It should attract the water and bend the stream towards it. Charges which are the same repel, or push each other away. So the balloon pushes away anything with the same charge as itself, such as another charged balloon. Write or draw what happens in your Science Record Book when you try out these experiments.

Battery Light Show

Kirsty has made a light show, to demonstrate how electricity works. Electricity is stored in the battery. It can only move, or flow, when it has a complete circle, or circuit, to go around. This circuit is made from wires, a switch and a bulb. When the switch is ON, the electricity goes from one end, or terminal, on the battery, along the wires, through the switch and light bulb, back to the battery's other terminal. As electricity goes through the bulb, it glows. When the switch is OFF, it makes a gap or break in the circuit. The electricity stops – and the light goes out.

Electric likes and dislikes

Electricity flows easily through some materials, like metals such as steel, iron and copper, and also water. These are called **conductors**. Electricity cannot flow through other things, like plastic, wood and pottery. These are called **insulators**. The wires in this experiment are made of metal on the inside, so the electricity can flow. The wire is covered with plastic to stop the electricity escaping.

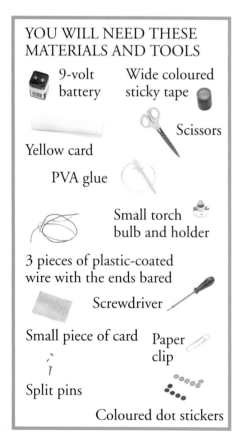

YOU WILL NEED THESE MATERIALS AND TOOLS

9-volt battery

Wide coloured sticky tape

Scissors

Yellow card

PVA glue

Small torch bulb and holder

3 pieces of plastic-coated wire with the ends bared

Screwdriver

Small piece of card

Paper clip

Split pins

Coloured dot stickers

! A 9-volt battery is perfectly safe for doing experiments. A grown-up should strip about 1 cm ($^1/_2$ in) of plastic from both ends of each piece of wire. Be careful how you screw the light bulb into its holder, since too much force may break the glass. Young children might need help with screws and screwdrivers.

WARNING

NEVER TOUCH ELECTRICAL WIRES, SWITCHES, PLUGS OR SOCKETS WITHOUT HELP FROM A GROWN-UP.

Kirsty switches the light on and off, showing how she can start and stop the electricity going around the circuit.

1 Decorate the battery to make it look powerful by winding a piece of wide coloured sticky tape right around it.

2 Cut out some zig-zag "lightning flashes" from the yellow card and stick them onto the sides of the battery with glue.

3 Screw the light bulb into the holder. Push the end of a piece of wire under one of the connecting screws. Screw it down. Repeat with another piece of wire under the other screw.

4 Take the end of one of these pieces of wire and twist it onto one of the battery terminals (the bits of metal on the top of the battery).

5 Twist the end of the third piece of wire onto the other battery terminal. Make sure that both these wires grip the terminals tightly.

6 Push two holes in the piece of card, the length of the paper clip apart. Push a split pin through one hole. Push the other split pin through the paper clip and then through the other hole. Open the ends of the pins under the card. This is the switch.

7 Twist one free wire end around one split pin and the other around the other split pin. When the paper clip touches both split pins, the switch is ON (green dot) and the light bulb shines. When the paper clip is moved away from the split pin, the switch is OFF (red dot).

23

Sound Skittles

Sound is caused by very fast to-and-fro movements in the air, called **vibrations**. When something makes a sound, invisible ripples or vibrations spread out through the air, like ripples in a pond, to your ears. These are called sound waves. The bigger the vibrations, the louder the sound. In this experiment, Liam shouts loudly into the sound cannon, to make the plastic sheet vibrate inside it. This vibrates the air inside the cannon. The sound waves come out of the hole at the end with such force that they knock over the skittles.

Liam is trying to knock all the skittles over with one blast of sound waves from his sound cannon.

Play a game

Stand your skittles in rows as in a 10-pin bowling alley – one in front, two behind, then three, and so on. Point the cannon at the skittles with the hole towards them. You can shout at the stretched plastic sheet of your cannon, or tap it with your fingers. How many skittles can you knock down in one go? You can play sound skittles with a friend. Hold the cannon behind a line and have three shouts each.

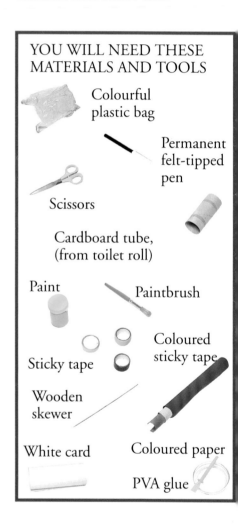

YOU WILL NEED THESE MATERIALS AND TOOLS

Colourful plastic bag

Permanent felt-tipped pen

Scissors

Cardboard tube, (from toilet roll)

Paint

Paintbrush

Sticky tape

Coloured sticky tape

Wooden skewer

White card

Coloured paper

PVA glue

The plastic sheets of the cannon must be taut, so a child might need help with stretching and sticking them. A grown-up should make the hole in the plastic sheet with a sharp point. The louder, shorter and sharper the sound used, the better the result.

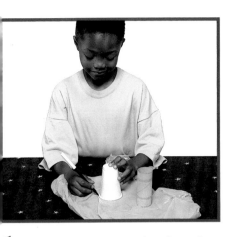

1 Draw two circles on the plastic bag about twice as big as the ends of the cardboard tube. Use another object as a guide. Use a permanent felt-tipped pen for this. Cut out the circles.

2 Paint the cardboard tube in a bright colour. You may need two coats of paint for a good effect. Leave to dry.

3 Fix the plastic circles tightly over the ends of the tube. You might need someone to help stretch the plastic tight, while you stick it with sticky tape.

4 Decorate the tube by winding coloured sticky tape around it, to make stripes.

5 Ask a grown-up to help you make a tiny hole with a skewer in the centre of one stretched plastic sheet at one end of the cannon.

6 Draw some skittle shapes on the white card. Cut out the skittles. Leave an extra bit on the bottom of each as a "foot".

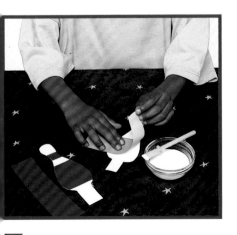

7 Decorate your skittles with stripes of coloured paper and sticky tape. Glue the paper onto the skittles.

8 Trim the coloured paper stripes to the same shape as the skittles with scissors. Bend the "feet" towards you.

Tumbler Telephone

Can you talk to a friend quietly, when he or she is at the other end of a big room? Liam's telephone works by sending the sound waves of his voice along the string. They go along the string as very fast to-and-fro movements called vibrations. When Liam talks into the tumbler or cup, the sound waves hit the bottom of the tumbler and make it vibrate. The vibrations pass along the string to the tumbler at the other end. They shake the bottom of this tumbler, which makes sound waves that go into Lorenzo's ear.

With his own tumbler telephone, Liam never gets a wrong number, and the lines are never busy. Also, his calls are always free!

Travelling waves

Sound waves travel well through air. They go through lots of other things too, such as water, wood, metals and glass. In fact, sound travels much faster and farther as vibrations in water, metals and glass, than it does through air. This is why whales and dolphins can "talk" to each other across huge distances in the ocean.

YOU WILL NEED THESE MATERIALS AND TOOLS

4 plastic tumblers or cups

Scissors

Felt-tipped pens

Coloured sticky tape

Coloured dot stickers

Skewer

Thin string

A friend to talk to!

! The tumbler telephone works well if the string is stretched quite tight and straight, and nothing touches it. Otherwise the vibrations cannot travel along it properly. The tumblers should be held by their rims only, so the bottoms are free to vibrate. Children may need help with cutting the tumblers and making holes with a sharp point.

1 Carefully cut the bottoms off two of the tumblers about 2 cm (³/₄ in) from the base. You may need to ask a grown-up to help you with this.

2 Stick a felt-tipped pen top to the bottom of each of the other two tumblers. These will be "aerials" – your telephones are like mobile ones!

3 Ask a grown-up to cut out small holes in the cut-off tumbler bottoms. Slip them neatly over the "aerials" to hold them in place.

4 Sticky-tape the cut-off bottoms in place. Add more stripes of sticky tape for decoration.

5 Make a "key pad" on each telephone with coloured dot stickers. Write numbers on the dots.

6 Ask a grown-up to make a tiny hole in the bottoms of the tumblers, with a skewer.

7 Thread the ends of the string through the holes in the telephones. Tie a large knot in each end of the string.

Chatting on the Telephone

Your friend walks away with one of the tumbler telephones, until the string is stretched tight, and holds the telephone to his or her ear. You speak into the telephone, and your friend listens. When you have finished talking, say "Over" like a real walkie-talkie user. Hold the telephone to your ear, to hear your friend's reply. Try using longer string to see if the telephone still works. Measure the greatest length and write the results in your Science Record Book.

Marvellous Mobiles

Air is all around us. We can not see it or touch it. But when it moves, we can feel it. Moving air comes from your mouth when you blow, and from a fan. The wind is moving air. Stand outside on a windy day and sometimes the moving air nearly knocks you over. Antonino's marvellous mobile swirls and twirls when moving air pushes it. You can find moving air around the house, such as near a window, door, radiator or table lamp.

Rising air

Indoors, moving air is sometimes called a draught, especially when it is cold and unwanted. Draughts in houses are caused by the wind blowing through gaps around windows or doors. Draughts are also caused in other ways. Hot air from a radiator or table lamp rises up to the ceiling, and makes a warm draught. On a cold night, cold air near a window falls to the floor as a cold draught.

> Children may need help with cutting and balancing the mobile. Hanging the mobile near any heat source, such as a radiator or lamp, must be supervised.

YOU WILL NEED THESE MATERIALS AND TOOLS

Pair of compasses

Pencil

Scissors

Coloured card

Sticky tape

Coloured sticky dots and stars

Thread or thin string

Wooden skewer

Antonino can use his marvellous mobile to detect wind, draughts and other moving air in his house.

1 Use the compasses to draw lots of circles on the coloured card. Make them any size but there must be two of each size.

2 Carefully cut out the circles using scissors. Arrange the discs in their equal-sized pairs.

3 Carefully cut a straight line or slit from the edge of each disc to its centre, where the compass point was.

4 Push the two discs of each pair together by their slits. Secure the joins with some sticky tape to make sure they hold together.

5 Decorate the discs with the coloured dots and stars.

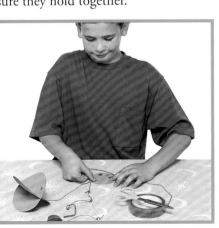

6 Cut the string or thread into different lengths. Stick one end of a string to the centre of each pair of discs. Tie the other end to the skewer.

A Mobile Draught-detector

Balance the mobile by moving the strings along the skewer until it does not tip over. Now, find places around the house where you can hang the mobile. If it turns or wobbles, you know there is air moving past it. Make a list of the places you test in your Science Record Book. Can you think what might cause the draughts?

Above: Tie another length of string to the centre of the skewer so you can hang it up.

Super Sail Boat

When air moves outside, it is called wind. Wind can be very powerful. Strong winds, called gales, blow down trees and damage buildings. People have used the power of the wind for thousands of years to push the sails of their boats, and travel across lakes, rivers and seas. Dean is going sailing too – with his super sail boat. You can make it move by producing your own wind, as you blow into the sail. Or you can sail it outdoors on a breezy day.

! Young children may need help cutting the plastic tumbler. A grown-up should push the skewer into the "boat". Outdoor sailing must always be supervised.

Dean blows his super sail boat across the "sea" to demonstrate the power of the wind.

Super sailors

The Ancient Egyptians, who built the Great Pyramids, discovered how to sail boats more than 5,000 years ago. As people learned more about sailing, they built bigger ships with more sails. Some great sailing ships had more than 30 sails! Today, most big ships are powered by engines that turn propellers. But many people still enjoy the sport of sailing and messing about in boats.

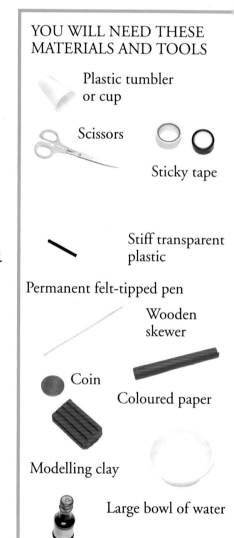

YOU WILL NEED THESE MATERIALS AND TOOLS

Plastic tumbler or cup

Scissors

Sticky tape

Stiff transparent plastic

Permanent felt-tipped pen

Wooden skewer

Coin

Coloured paper

Modelling clay

Large bowl of water

Food colouring, blue or green

1 Carefully cut an oval hole in the side of a plastic cup – you can cut through the rim. You may need to ask a grown-up to help with this.

2 Repair the cut rim, and make the boat stronger at the same time, by putting two or three layers of sticky tape all round the rim.

3 Draw around the rim of the cup onto the transparent plastic. Use a permanent felt-tipped pen for this. Ordinary felt-tip ink may rub off.

4 Cut out the circle. Tape it firmly over the rim of the cup to make the back end of your boat.

5 Stick extra tape firmly around the rim of the cup. This makes sure the boat will not leak.

6 Ask a grown-up to push the skewer through the bottom of the boat. It is both the mast above the boat, and the keel underneath in the water.

7 Cut a sail from coloured paper. Ask a grown-up to make two holes in it, top and bottom, and thread it onto the skewer mast. Sticky-tape a coin to the keel.

8 Push the skewer up, so the coin is against the bottom. Fix it in place with modelling clay. Add some blue or green food colouring to the water or "sea" in the bowl.

Sailing Forwards, and Sideways

The sail works best if it is slightly curled, like Dean's. The coin on the keel will keep the boat upright. When you blow the boat, which way does the sail turn to catch the wind? Make the boat go straight across the water to the other side. Can you make the boat go sideways? Try twisting the sail around on the mast. This will make the boat go in a different direction.

Hold Water Upside Down!

This famous trick looks impossible, or perhaps it is magic. Can you really hold water in an upside-down tumbler? Yes, Antonino shows that it truly does work. It depends on science. The force that pulls you, a cat, a chair and everything else in the world, down towards the ground, is called gravity. Gravity tries to make the water fall out of the upside-down tumbler towards the ground. But in this trick, air keeps the water in the tumbler.

Heavy air

Air has weight, although it does not weigh much. There is a lot of it pressing on us, since there is a huge amount of air high above. We do not notice this pressing force, because we are used to it. It is called **air pressure**, and it is this that keeps the water in the glass. The water is trapped inside the glass by the card. Air presses down, around and up underneath the card, holding it in place, and keeping the water inside the tumbler.

YOU WILL NEED THESE MATERIALS AND TOOLS

Large bowl of water

Food colouring

Plastic tumbler

Pencil

Thick, smooth, shiny, flat card

Scissors

! This experiment involves a lot of water and does not always work right first time. So it should be performed in a suitable waterproof area. Use a plastic tumbler and bowl rather than glass ones, for safety. We have used glass ones here so you can see how the experiment works. Clean, smooth, shiny, flat card is best. The experiment works less well if the card becomes soggy or bent. Children may need help cutting the card.

It looks like magic. But Antonino is using the science of air, water and gravity to stop his feet getting wet!

1 Add a little food colouring to the water in the bowl and stir it around. This is so you can see the water inside the tumbler.

2 Draw around the rim of the tumbler onto the card. Then draw a square around this circle, about 2 cm (³/₄ in) larger than the circle all around.

3 Carefully cut out the square of card. It should fit easily over the top of the tumbler, with plenty of extra card around the rim.

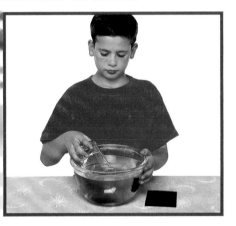

4 Put the tumbler into the bowl of water. Hold it under, with the open end pointing up. Make sure that it fills up completely.

5 Make sure there are no bubbles of air inside the tumbler, by tapping it. The trick will not work if there is any air in the tumbler.

6 Turn the tumbler upside down. Lift it partly out, but keep the rim under the water. Slide the card into the water and under the rim.

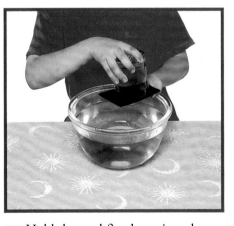

7 Hold the card firmly against the rim of the beaker. Slowly lift the card and beaker, still upside down, out of the water.

8 Hold the tumbler upside down and level. Without sliding the card, take your other hand away from the card.

Air, Water and Weather

The layer of air all around the Earth is called the atmosphere. Air's weight changes when it gets hot or cold, and these changes cause our weather. When air is warmed by the sun, it rises higher. Cooler air moves along to take its place. This is wind. As air rises, the invisible moisture in it turns to tiny drops of water. These make clouds. As the drops get bigger, they fall as rain.

Sink or Swim

Water is very strong. It can push things. When it flows in rivers, or in sea currents, it pushes objects along. Water also pushes down all the time, because it is very heavy. But it also pushes up, too. This upwards pushing is called upthrust, and it makes things float. Izabella is discovering that water's upthrust is strong enough to support some things and make them float, but that others are too heavy and sink.

Floating forces

An object floats if the upwards push of the water, called **upthrust,** is more than the downwards push of the object. The downwards push of the object is called **displacement** because it moves aside (dis-places) some water. An object that is small for its weight, like a pebble, displaces only a small amount of water. So it sinks. If an object is large for its weight, like a sponge, it floats.

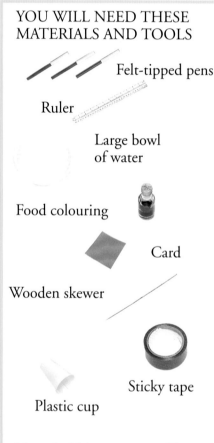

YOU WILL NEED THESE MATERIALS AND TOOLS

Felt-tipped pens

Ruler

Large bowl of water

Food colouring

Card

Wooden skewer

Sticky tape

Plastic cup

Household items or toys like a cork, pumice stone, pebble, small sieve, metal dish, clothes peg, dry sponge, paper clip, wooden spoon, metal spoon, nail, piece of polystyrene, table-tennis ball, and so on.

❗ Do not use glass or sharp objects in this experiment. A suitable waterproof area is essential.

Izabella tests some household things to see if they sink or float in water. You could try lots of other objects too.

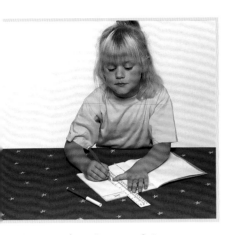

1 Draw a chart in your Science Record Book with three columns. In the first column, write the names or draw the items you will test. The middle column is for those that SWIM. The last is for those that SINK.

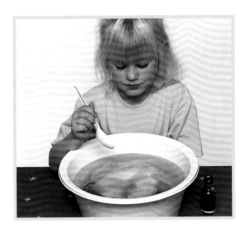

2 Ask a grown-up to fill a large bowl of water. Stir in some food colouring – just for fun!

3 Make a float-marker by cutting out a sail shape from the piece of card. Tape it to a wooden skewer. Ask a grown up to push the skewer into the bottom of a plastic cup. Half-fill the cup with water and float it.

4 Put the cork, the pumice stone and the pebble on the surface of the water. Do they sink or swim?

5 Put a cross in the SINK or a tick in the SWIM column of your Science Record Book for each item.

6 Try to float the small sieve and the metal dish. Put the results in your Science Record Book.

7 Test a clothes peg and the sponge. Leave the sponge in the water for a long time. Does it still float as high?

Weight, Shape and Water

If something has air in it, like the dry sponge, it weighs less. So it is likely to float. The metal dish also has air "in" it when it is the right way up, so it floats too. This is how metal boats float. If the air is replaced by water, the object becomes heavier and it may sink. This is why the sponge gradually floats lower as it soaks up water. Tip over the dish and it fills with water and sinks. This is what happens when a boat capsizes. The float-marker is half full of water and half full of air, so it half floats. Pumice stone is bubbly rock full of air that is made by volcanoes.

The Great Iceberg Puzzle

One of the great puzzles of nature is how icebergs float. Icebergs are huge lumps of ice that drift about in the cold seas near the North and South Poles. Some icebergs are bigger than cities. They weigh thousands of tonnes. As water gets colder, it gets heavier. So cold water sinks below warm water. Icebergs are frozen water and so are even colder. So why do they not sink to the bottom of the sea? Lorenzo finds out why in this experiment, by using tiny icebergs from a refrigerator or freezer. They will work the same as a real iceberg, but they are much smaller!

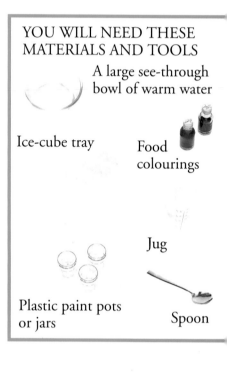

Lorenzo has made lots of coloured "icebergs". He is investigating how they float and then melt.

YOU WILL NEED THESE MATERIALS AND TOOLS

A large see-through bowl of warm water

Ice-cube tray

Food colourings

Jug

Plastic paint pots or jars

Spoon

Light ice

As water gets colder, it becomes heavier. But this only happens down to the temperature of 4°C (40°F). If it gets colder than that, it begins to get lighter again and so rises towards the surface. When it cools to 0°C (32°F), liquid water freezes into solid ice. This cold ice is quite light and it floats on water. This means that animals and plants which live in water do not have to freeze solid themselves when the temperature drops to or below freezing. They can survive in the cold water below the ice that floats on ponds and lakes.

1 Make some mini-icebergs by putting food colouring into some water in paint pots or jars. You can make them in several different colours, but do not mix the colours together.

2 Spoon the coloured water carefully into the ice-cube tray or other containers, if you wish. Put this into a freezer or the freezing compartment of a refrigerator. Leave until frozen solid.

3 When the ice-cubes are frozen, fill the large bowl with warm water. Ask a grown-up to help you with this. Then remove the ice-cube tray from the freezer or refrigerator.

4 Drop coloured ice-cubes into the water. Watch what happens. Do they sink? Look at the bowl from the side. Can you see the ice melting? What does it do?

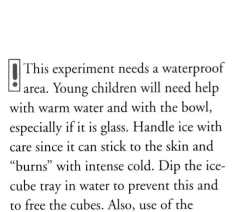

This experiment needs a waterproof area. Young children will need help with warm water and with the bowl, especially if it is glass. Handle ice with care since it can stick to the skin and "burns" with intense cold. Dip the ice-cube tray in water to prevent this and to free the cubes. Also, use of the freezer must always be supervised.

Underwater Fountain

You can investigate how warm water floats and cold water sinks by making an underwater fountain. Fill a large bowl with cold water. Then fill a small plastic bottle with warm water. (The plastic bottle must be small enough to sink below the surface of the water in the bowl.) Add some food colouring to it. Carefully lower the bottle into the bowl and make it sit on the bottom. Does the warm coloured water stay in the bottle? Where does it go? Draw a picture of your fountain in your Science Research Book to show your results. You could also try dropping in some coloured ice-cubes, made with a different food colouring, into the water. The ice is lighter than the water around it, so it floats. The warmer water melts the coloured ice. But the coloured water that comes from the ice is colder and heavier than the water, so it sinks. Look very carefully to see the cold, coloured water trickling from the iceberg and sinking to the bottom.

Kitchen Chemistry

Everything in the world is made of chemicals. Some are artificial chemicals, like those made in factories. Others are natural chemicals, like those in your own body and in the rocks and soil. Even the food you eat is made of chemicals. Scientists who study chemicals are called chemists. You can be a kitchen chemist, like Dean, and study the chemicals in the cupboard. Cooking is a form of chemistry. You mix together the chemicals and make them join together, or react, to form a tasty snack.

The acid test

Some cooking substances, like vinegar or lemon juice, are sour. They are called **acidic**. Other kitchen substances, like bicarbonate of soda (bicarb), are slightly slimy and bitter. They are called **basic** or **alkali**. Bases are the opposite of acids. Chemists often need to know whether chemicals are acids or bases. If they do not know what the chemicals are, they should never taste them to find out, because many chemicals are poisonous. So chemists make special substances called **chemical indicators**, to test them. Red cabbage water is a good chemical indicator to tell the difference between acids and bases.

! Young children must be supervised in the kitchen, as some foods and liquids can cause sickness in large quantities. Chopping and boiling the cabbage should always be done by a grown-up.

Dean has put a strip of blotting paper into each of his test jars. The name of the test juice or liquid is marked on the paper in pencil. He can then let the strips dry and clip them into his Science Record Book.

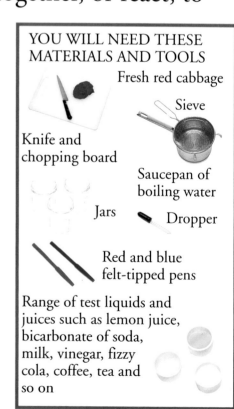

YOU WILL NEED THESE MATERIALS AND TOOLS

Fresh red cabbage

Knife and chopping board

Sieve

Saucepan of boiling water

Jars

Dropper

Red and blue felt-tipped pens

Range of test liquids and juices such as lemon juice, bicarbonate of soda, milk, vinegar, fizzy cola, coffee, tea and so on

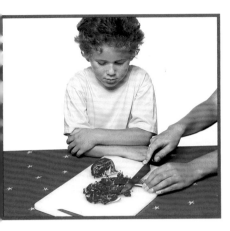

1 Ask a grown-up to chop the cabbage, put it into boiling water for about 15 minutes, then strain the water through a sieve.

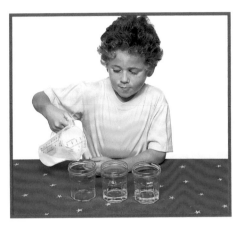

2 While the chemical indicator (the red cabbage water) is cooling, put a little tap water into each jar. Get your Science Record Book ready.

3 Add about 15 drops of the chemical indicator to each jar, using the dropper. Look at the colour and note it in your Science Record Book.

Recording Your Results

Colour in the result of each experiment in your Science Record Book. Draw three columns. In the first column, write the name or draw a picture of the test substance. In the second column put a mark for those that turned red or orange with a red felt-tipped pen. In the third column put a mark for those that turned purple or blue with a blue felt-tipped pen. Acids join or react with the red cabbage water to turn it red or orange. Bases do the same but turn it purple or blue. During the experiment, keep one jar that contains just the chemical indicator. Scientists call this a "control". You can compare the colour changes in the other jars with the original colour in the "control" jar.

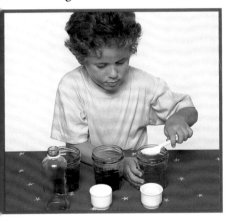

4 Add one test liquid to a jar, such as a spoonful of juice squeezed from a lemon. Stir it in. Watch and note down any colour change.

5 Add another test liquid, such as a spoonful of milk, to the next jar. As before, mix it, and note down any colour change in your book.

6 Add the next test liquid, such as a few drops of vinegar, to the next jar. Note any change. Do this with the other test liquids and juices.

Vinegar Volcano

What happens when acids and bases, or alkalis, meet? Kirsty has made a peaceful-looking tropical island, but it is about to get shaken by a huge volcano. She can make the volcano explode or erupt using simple chemicals – the acid vinegar and the base bicarbonate of soda. The spectacular effect is caused by the reaction between the acid and the base. The food colouring makes it look like real, red-hot, runny rock.

YOU WILL NEED THESE MATERIALS AND TOOLS

Red food colouring

Vinegar

2 small plastic or glass bottles

Funnel

Bicarbonate of soda (bicarb)

Large blue plate

Sand

PVA glue

Coloured paper

Pencil

Scissors

Coloured sticky tape

Fizzy gas

Everything is made of chemicals. And all chemicals are made of tiny particles called **atoms**. During a chemical reaction, the groups of atoms are taken apart, mixed and shuffled, then joined together in different groups, to make new chemicals. When vinegar is mixed with bicarbonate of soda (bicarb), one of the new chemicals formed is a gas. The bubbles of this gas make the volcano fizz.

This chemical reaction is not dangerous. The gas produced is carbon dioxide, but with the recommended quantities of vinegar and bicarbonate of soda (bicarb), its amounts are very small and not harmful. However, the child should be supervised in case of spillage.

Kirsty's vinegar volcanic island is based on a simple chemical reaction. A real volcano is millions of times more powerful, and based on heat and pressure.

1 Add some red food colouring to some vinegar in a small bottle using the funnel.

2 Wash and dry the funnel. Use it to put 1 or 2 dessert spoons of bicarb into another small bottle.

3 Stand this bottle in the middle of the plate as the volcano. Pile the sand around it.

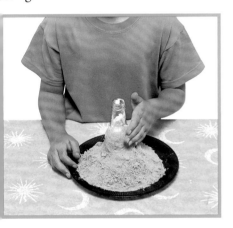

4 Paint the sides of the bottle with glue, to make it stick. Leave the bottle's mouth clear. This is the volcano's opening, or crater.

5 Make a palm tree. Draw some leaves on green paper and cut them out. Snip around their edges to make fronds. Roll up some coloured paper to make the tree trunk.

6 Tape round the top and bottom of the trunk and cut it off square, so it stands up. Tape the palm leaf shapes to the top of the trunk.

7 Using the funnel, carefully pour some of the coloured vinegar onto the bicarb in the bottle on the island, and quickly remove the funnel.

Lots of Eruptions

The red, bubbly "lava" fizzes out of the top of the volcano. The chemical reaction starts as soon as the vinegar mixes with the bicarb. When the volcano has finished erupting, stir inside the bottle with a skewer and pour in some more vinegar. You may get several eruptions in this way.